"Love is Bullsh*t" is a collection of poems written and independently published by Mariguelle. First Edition, 2023.

Published by Mariguelle

ISBN: 978-1-958066-26-3

Table of Contents

Message from the Author

Dedication

A Mistake After All

I'm Still His

Mixed Signals

A Love Like This

How I Wish

You're Finally Free

Haunted

Don't Tell Me

Not All I Love You Is True

I

How?

Hidden Letter for Mom

Broken Promises

Healing

Help

How Come You Can't See Me

You

Longing

What If…

Agony and Ecstasy

Serial Killer

You Are a Masterpiece

I Will Never Have You

Silent Screams

Unrequited Love

Love Just Isn't Enough

Celebrating Christmas Alone

I Miss You

A Blissful Beginning, An Unfortunate End

She

Grieve

An Apology Letter for You

Heartbreak

Love Heals

Love Again

Power of Love

Love is True

Acknowledgments

Message from the Author

Dear Readers,

I am the author of the book you hold in your hands, a collection of poems that explore the themes of cheating and heartbreak. These poems come from my own experiences and I hope that they will touch your heart in some way.

Although some of the poems may be raw and painful, I believe that love is a powerful force that can heal us and bring us hope. It is my sincere wish that you find comfort, healing, and even a glimmer of hope as you read my words.

Thank you for taking the time to read my book. I hope it will bring you as much joy as it did for me to write it.

Wishing you love and peace,

Mariguelle

Dedication

To my mother, who has been my rock and my source of inspiration through all of life's ups and downs.

To my friends, who have been there for me and encouraged me to share my voice and my story through poetry.

And to all those who have experienced heartbreak and betrayal, I dedicate this book to you. May my words bring you comfort and remind you that you are not alone in your journey.

A Mistake After All

I was left wondering why

How that beautiful hello ended up with a traumatic
goodbye

Sure, do people often come and go

I just wish I knew it was you though

How can you look me directly in my eyes

When you knew all along—you were just telling me lies

It was too regretful to recall

Had I only realized you were a mistake after all

I'm Still His

You loved me right from the start

Patiently picking up these pieces that keep on falling apart

Baby, here you are in front of me

You're all that I need which I'm failing to see

I wish I can make you feel the same

I hope I can mean every I love you, every time I say your name

But baby, I am still his even if he'll say no

Even if he did already let me go

I can't just leave this familiar home

Even at this moment that I am writing this poem

Will you still be there if it would take me quite some time?

'Cause baby, I'm still his, even he's no longer mine

Mixed Signals

Said we love each other on both ends

But it's only I who made it in the middle

Felt like we were less than lovers but more than

friends

With all of those hints and cues of yours

that's subtle

I'm growing tired of this catch and chase

I'm so over this guessing game you want to play

I'm tired of this heavy heart, unclear thoughts

and all of your inconsistencies

Just stop saying you love me when it felt like the

other way

If you can't love me whole- this is then the end

of us

I deserve clarity, honesty, love, and green flags

If it's something you'll choose not to give

This ain't the right lifetime for both of us to live.

A Love Like This

I haven't felt this kind of love before
Everything's new, the taste, the color
I didn't know a love like this exists
In this world incapable of it.

But here you are shining in front of me
Making me feel and once again see
I felt alive with this heart of mine beating
And just suddenly, you and I meant
everything.

Today I offer you my faithfulness
A love that's real, raw, and honest
A love that's true in a world full of lies
A love that won't end even if this body dies.

How I Wish

I would never listen to music again

I do not want to hear another melody

From that moment I heard your voice

It was the sound of perfection

Love and pain one in rhythm

I wish to always remember what it's like

I would die to just hear it one more time

How I wish,

How I wish I can make you mine.

You're Finally Free

I'll set you free, I'll let you go
Dear love of my life, please go.

Haunted

And that night we shared together

With your arms around me

And your head on my chest

Everything was perfect.

But I haven't known

That those memories will haunt me

During these days when I feel the most lonely

I still long for your love, even if you broke me.

Don't Tell Me

Don't tell me how much of you I am allowed to love

Don't tell me how long I should stay by your side

It is not for you to decide

This love that I feel is beyond the test of time

A love that will remain even if you're no longer mine

Not All I Love You Is True

Don't believe what they always say

Take notice of what they do

Cause baby, not all I love you is true.

I

It was you and I

In our own ride or die

You've seen me laugh and heard me cry

We've been through a lot now I'm left asking why

If it's meant for us two

Why is there only I

It's now only I

At the end of the road, thought I still got you by my side

But baby now there's only I

In our own ride or die.

How?

How do you make it through each day with a heavy heart,
broken and bleeding?

How do you continue living when you feel like you're close
to dying with each breath?

Hidden Letter for Mom

I am no longer that kid that when she cries is just in need of candy

I am now 23 with a wounded heart and can't tell you directly

I've fallen in love mom and was hurt deeply

I am in the process of healing and I hope there's something you can tell me.

I am no longer afraid of monsters

I am now afraid of love.

Love is scary, mom.

Broken Promises

I was once too promised of all the good things

I was once too hopeful and excited

I witnessed how I looked forward but saw everything
shattered

I am too a victim of broken promises...

Healing

The moment your heart stops beating

Your mind will start working

It may be painful still

But that my dear is the start of the process called healing.

Help

Silent screams

Shapeless pain

Hidden tears

Streamin' down over and over again

How Come You Can't See Me

You've seen me naked

You've seen me whole

I let you see my soul

A love that's long and lasting

That's how I've seen it

And so, I've given my all.

You

Your heart

Is the most beautiful piece of art

Your mind

Are the celestial bodies all combined

Your body

Is a temple I'll worship every single day

Your soul, your spirit, your whole being

You are whom I've prayed for

You are my dream come true

And if forever does exist, I will spend it loving you.

Longing

In the silence of the night, I lay awake, thinking of the times when your lips were pressed against mine, and the feeling of your arms around me, holding me close, keeping me warm, and at that moment, I knew that there was nowhere else in the world that I would rather be than in your embrace.

And as I think back to those moments, I can't help but feel a longing for that feeling of completeness and wholeness.

What If...

What if we had never met
And our paths never crossed
Would my life be empty yet
Or somehow be less lost?

What if I had never fallen
In love with you so deep
Would I be standing tall
Or be lost in endless sleep?

What if we had fought harder
To keep our love alive
Would the flames of passion fonder
Or simply wither and die?

What if we had held on tight
To the love that we once shared
Would the darkness of the night
Have left us feeling scared?

What if we had fought for us

And not let fear consume

Would our love be stronger thus

Or forever succumb?

Agony and Ecstasy

Her mind is a buzz

Creating a symphony

I am in love with her thoughts

Her ideas, her intention, her curiosity.

Her heart is a beat

A rhythm all on its own

I am drawn, enchanted by its melody

It fills me with comfort, warmth, and safety.

Her soul is a song

A beautiful refrain

I am delighted by its music

But now fills my heart with pain.

She's fortune and tragedy

A complex and beautiful entity

The paradox of life

The dueling agony and ecstasy.

Serial Killer

I don't know if I should ask you this
I don't know if I'm prepared for it
Whatever you'll answer is
It's gonna dictate my fate

A simple yes or no
Could mean life or death
Between holding on and letting go
Lies my last breath

I feared this day would come
That I'll hate life I've learned to love
Things I'd like would start to hurt
Fvck all music, fvck all art

Damn rainbows and unicorns
Damn fairy tales and happy endings
All I have is a hope forlorn
And I don't wanna be saved either
Let me die with these tears that'll never stop falling

A heart that'll bleed forever

Let this story be known as a reminder

That true love could sometimes be a disguised serial killer

You Are a Masterpiece

Your heart

Is the most beautiful piece of art

Your mind

Are the celestial bodies all combined

Your body

Is a temple I'll worship every single day

Your soul, your spirit, your whole being

You are whom I prayed for

You are my dream come true

And if forever does exist, I will spend it loving you

I Will Never Have You

I try to tell myself it's time to move on

That our love was just a temporary dawn

But every time I see your face— my heart starts to race

I still love you, even though you don't love me in the same
place

Seeing you with someone else hurts so deep

I wonder if you ever think of me— if you ever sleep

I wonder if you ever think of me

Or if I'm just a distant memory

I miss the way you used to hold me tight

The way you'd look at me with love in your eyes

But now all I have are these painful memories

Of a love that was once so sweet— but now just tortures
me

I know I should move on, and find someone new

But every time I try— my thoughts always lead back to you

I still love you, despite the pain

I love you and it hurts knowing that you don't feel the same

I will always love you still

Even if I will never have you again.

Silent Screams

The pain I feel cuts so deep

But no one hears the silent screams I keep

I hide my hurt, I mask the pain

But deep inside, my heart is driving me insane

I try to laugh, I try to smile

But the weight of it all is more than I can bear for a while

So, I suffer in silence, I bear it all alone

Hoping one day, I'll find my way home

But until then, I'll keep on going

Hiding the pain, that no one is knowing

For I am strong and I'll find a way

To deal with this pain, even if it's killing me each and
every day.

Unrequited Love

I see you every day, my love unspoken
My feelings for you, forever unbroken
But you don't see me, you don't even know
The love I have for you continues to grow

I love you more than words can say
But you're out of reach, so far away
You're in other arms, with another love
And all I can do is look up above

I love you from afar, with all my heart
But I know you can't love me back from the very start
I love you still, from a distance true
But I think it's time to let this go
I'll find love, that's meant for me
And leave behind, this love that couldn't be

Love Just Isn't Enough

I never wanted to let you go
But sometimes love just isn't enough, I know
We loved each other, with all our hearts
But now the time has come, for us to part

The pain is overwhelming, the tears never end
But we both know, this love has to bend
We have to let each other go, even though it hurts
Even if the pain is tearing me apart

We'll always have the memories, of the love we knew
But it's time to say goodbye, and start anew
You know how much I love you
Even if it means letting you go
Even if I don't want to
It's hard to do
It's hard to say
But we both know, it's the only way.

Celebrating Christmas Alone

Oblivious of what lies ahead
I felt stupid, I was dumbfounded
I thought everything was real, everything was true
I was blind, I thought that you love me too.

Was it fun watching me walk on your palm?
Letting me feel unbelievably calm
You held my arms; you kept me warm
I felt safe, little did I know that all you meant was harm.

You did exactly what I told you would hurt me the most
I fell in your trap; I admit I have lost
A game it is, when I thought it was love
What a perfect gift, this season, that I could have.

In the most wonderful time of the year
You only brought me so much pain and endless tears
Had you as my fortress, my stronghold, my home
Surprisingly, I am now left celebrating Christmas alone.

I Miss You

As I lay my head down on your chest, hear your heart beating— it was the most wonderful music I'll never get tired of listening to.

Drowning with your warm breath, enchanted with your scent— a fragrance I won't be able to forget.

It's haunting me, all of you, it's coming after all these broken pieces. Vision of myself buried on your neck— lost in every kisses.

I've lost my power before your body— a temple I once kneeled, adored and worshipped.

Your gasps, your arms behind my back, my name falling off your lips— it's all still clear in my memory.

Damn, I miss you already.

A Blissful Beginning, An Unfortunate End

It's a bliss that we're able to meet

Got to know each for a couple of weeks

You're someone I pretty much adore

Which makes me want to know you more.

It was rainbows, unicorns, and sunshine

The very moment your path crossed mine

We laughed, we bonded, missed each other after every
goodbye

Little did we know how fast the days pass by.

I haven't heard from you for quite some time

You've been gone for a little long while

I haven't seen even your ghost

You left me puzzled, hanging, and lost

With questions, I wondered and pondered

I ask alone in this world of uncharted

How did we even come to an end

Right before we even started?

She

She's not the type of girl that you can think of

She thinks she's weird, clumsy, and not worthy of love

There's this gloomy storm following her all day round

She's a hurricane, she floods and she had me badly
drowned.

I have had my eyes set on her from the day we conversed

From her gaze and her face, I've seen the whole universe

I want to outshine the darkness surrounding her

I have this desire of wanting to treat her better.

I dream of her every day and every night

Unable to endure the wait to have her mine

Till I realized just a few days ago,

Loving her just means letting her go

Wanting her feels so wrong

'Coz she's not meant to be mine all along.

Grieve

I'm throwing the pen now, I'm ending this story

You'll no longer be present in my next journey

So let me enjoy this coffee now, on this grave where I sit

Watching your character die

While I'm burning all the chapters with your name in it.

An Apology Letter for You

This is how I express what I feel
In isolation and with a bucket of beer
Speaking in all honesty, keeping everything real
Here are the words I want you to hear

We were talking earlier that day
Talked about us, what are we
Asked why am I again not ready
Said you're willing to wait
You're too patient and I can't even give you a date

Truth is, I'm lost and I don't want to be found still
I may scream for help but I can't leave this place here
The pain, heartache, and all that's haunting me
At some point, I enjoy their company

And so, I allowed you to see me in the abyss
I showed you my flaws and imperfections
I've let you meet the devil in me
Yet you found beauty in it

I pushed you away

I almost do it every single day

But you never missed a chance to remind me that you're
here to stay

I'm unstable, unsure and I embodied insanity

How come you've ignored it and adored me anyway

I want to feel loved

And you're giving it

I am treated the way I always wanted

But it kinda feels like I don't deserve it

I can lie to myself as much as I can

But I have to accept that this ain't still the right time

I don't want to lose you though

But I can't have you stay

How can I want you for myself and not at the same time

I want you to find somebody else but I want you to be mine

I am broken and my edges are sharp

You'll end up bleeding even before we start

You even remained true to everything you've said

You're so green baby while I'm burning in red.

This is my inner child speaking

I still seek healing

It's not something that you can help me with

It's something that I must do

And I owe you an apology, for letting you in just to let you go.

Heartbreak

Heartbreak is the feeling of loss and longing, of emptiness and despair. It's the knowledge that something you once held so dear is now gone, and the realization that it may never come back. It's the tears that fall without warning, the nights spent tossing and turning, and the days that feel endless and gray.

Love Heals

In the end, it is that love that will help us heal and move forward, stronger and wiser for the experience.

Love Again

Heartbreak is a heartache that consumes, but also a chance for growth and self-discovery. A reminder to hold onto hope and love again.

Power of Love

Through the pain you'll intensely feel in a breakup only,
one will truly understand the depth and power of love, and
emerges stronger, with a deeper capacity to love again.

Love is True

Love is true and unwavering, and although heartache and pain may come, the love we truly deserve will always find its way to us.

Acknowledgments

This book would not have been possible without the support of my family and friends who have been with me through the darkest moments of my life. I would like to extend my deepest gratitude to those who have encouraged me to put my experiences into words, providing me with the strength to be vulnerable and truthful in my poetry.

I also want to thank all those who have bravely shared their own stories of heartbreak, reminding me that I am not alone in my struggles. Your courage has inspired me to create this collection, in the hope that it might offer solace and comfort to others who have been through similar experiences.

Finally, I want to express my immense appreciation to everyone who has read this book and who has been moved by my words. It is my sincerest wish that this collection will serve as a reminder of the power of healing and growth, even in the face of the greatest pain and heartache.

www.ingramcontent.com/pod-product-compliance
Lightning Source LLC
Chambersburg PA
CBHW051559120626
46551CB00013B/1589